So This Is It

David R Mellor

CONTENTS

ONE HAGIA SOPHIA

To walk and see…
Christ's outstretched hand
Calling you to his side.
Mingling with the Koran
Declaring god's love to those
Who carry him inside

Prayers that have echoed
In this chamber for centuries
Christian and Muslim cemented in the walls
To remind us…
That faith is not war

But now the veil has fallen…
Christ's eyes hidden
Turning his back in shame.
As now the Mosque is open,
And my faith is silenced

TURNING DARKNESS TO LIGHT (FOR LEONARD COHEN)

Broken, turning to the arm of the record player
resting down the crackling voice
telling you what you have just been through
and will do again, and you are not alone.

And the words seep in like a porous sponge
just wanting to be healed and protected

and you carry his armour
of a trilby hat
not so fitting suit
a smile that would fit perfectly on a child

dent the slinging arrows
and barbed words
that come your way

and trickle slowly down the rainy street
singing his words

A SPECK OF CRUELTY (A TRUE STORY ABOUT A DEAR OLD NEIGHBOUR OF MINE)

One tiny story
One tiny life
Not picked up on any radar
Or satellite

Not even
A marking in a road
Or unfortunately
No CCTV

Old Ray's tools were stolen
From his ransacked allotment
Leaving
Very little of him left .

One tiny moment
One tiny heartless mind
Just started to bury him
Further
And further
In the ground

DEATH IN PARADISE (TESTIMONY OF A WITNESSED EVENT)

A body falls…
Men dive in
Phones ring out
Faces look shocked
The ambulance arrives…
A dead body is put inside

And the corner shop is
Open…
We put the beer in the bag
Hope the water is back on
Plan the telly

…

As an ambulance speeds by
Under a milky moon

Back home…
the neighbour
Brushed by…
his brother had drowned
and died

AS I GET OLDER ...

The memories
become more painful

you would think…
 so far from the source
that they would have faded to a
dot.

But they shine brighter …
Than the first inflicted blows

Like a mosquito
Bloated on blood
Saving themselves

Til now

I AM MY OWN WORST ENEMY

I am my own
Worst enemy
Perfectly made by you…

Seasoned with temper
Peppered with self-loathing
Add a dash of despondency

And there I go…

I am my own worst enemy
Perfectly made into you .

THE DAILY COUNT OF LIVES

746   (six fell in love more than four times)

673   (twenty had no regrets)

714   (five could still feel their first kiss)

643   (twenty-seven looked at photos of their loved one
each morning)

547   (seven had contagious laughter)

517   (hundred regretted that their beauty had faded)

468   (thirty-five had worked in the same job all their lives)

573   (eight had won awards for their service to others)

375   (seventy-five had been broken hearted)

817   (had touched a million souls)

917   (all had been loved by someone)

Behind every **number**...

WE LIVE BY THE HANDS OF OTHERS

We live by the hands of others
Not seen by you or me

They pass the parcel
Stand at the till
Nurse the wounded
Or keep order

We live by the hands of others
Not seen by you or me

Our hands scrubbed clean and safe

But…

We live by and are grateful to others
Who have to live day by day with that terrible fear

THIS MORTAL LIFE

This mortal life
Seems thinner now

As we move away from
The old and sick relatives

Keep a safe distance
See everyone as a potential disease

This moral life
Seems thinner now

And in a darkened room, all alone
She sits tapping her fingers ,
Hoping the bell will ring
Or someone will call

Her mortal life
Thinner now
Passing away
All alone

A THREADBARE YEAR

A Threadbare year
Still too hot to touch
    Those that were poor
    Remain so
    Those full of hope
    Chocked on feathers

Ballot Boxes
Full of X defeating Y

Why this thread of decency and kindness
Has become a dye
Faded like a hippy t shirt
Folded away neatly
To decay and die

Instead they are puffed up bloated
And the I I I and 'we' will make our country great again
No matter how many
Fall by the wayside

A threadbare year
Still to hot to touch
Will there be anything left of it
this time next year

THE SUN COMING THROUGH A MURKY WINDOW

The sun coming through a murky window
 might not seem like perfection to you …
 it may be run of the mill

but to me it spells
no more returning to the cruelty of work
which soaked my skin with anxiety
no more dripping at the bus stop
and waiting …
to be sentenced to death
for not completing this or that form

The sun coming through a murky window
Is a blessing I never saw before
My eyes closed…
Now open
Without you

NO SOUND

and soon the bombs won't fall
and soon the bombs will start again
and soon the child will sleep
and soon the child will not sleep again
and soon she will put her arms around her father
and soon she will lay him in the ground
and now the screams of agony from the child
echo back with no sound

TIME WASTED, TIME WASTED, TIME WASTED ME

I didn't realise how bad life could be
Until I realised I was me
Naked in front of the mirror
Bulges where there shouldn't be

Time wasted, time wasted, time wasted me

I didn't realise how quickly the clock of time could
Cover me, leave me, breathless, and not
how it should be

Me up a tree
Me with you Carl creating Marvel figures before tea

Time wasted, time wasted, time wasted me

And you my father and mother feckless and insecure
Gave me a back bone of a cripple always to spend my life on the
bottom of the sea, for sure

Time wasted, time wasted, time wasted you and me

TAKE ME HOME

I'm waiting for the bus
To drive me home
So that I can cry alone

Leaving behind
A beautiful face

One I trace now…
On the…
back of this leather seat
knowing that there's nothing that can bring you back

just…
Waiting…
for the bus…

To drive me home

So that I won't be alone
With words that we're though

Ticket collector stares
at my watery eyes
Counting out the pennies
and feeling rather lost…
Without your hand, your smile, your ways, your touch
nothing in life felt too much
that'll be £3.75 please

EVERY DAY I SAY GOODBYE TO MYSELF

Little bits get loose and flaky
And disappear, like memories of what I did today
Or who I should have been all those yesterdays

Every day I say goodbye,
To a little of myself

My age is now my waist line
My vision that of an unborn
There is no way of stopping the clocks
Which seem to spin faster
Than when I hit that football

Every day I say goodbye,
Every day I say goodbye, to you me
And the little of myself that is still left inside

HE WASN'T MY FATHER

He wasn't my dad
But I thought he was…

Hunched up at the bar
Cracking jokes
Stealing the show

I felt like tapping him on the shoulder
And telling him
"I have so much to tell you."

But the words lay as flat as the beer I had just bought

And the lost words we had never spoken
Built up in the ashtray
Are gulped by the beers

And the distant murmur of cars
Signaled, goodbye…

I TURN DOWN A BLIND ALLEY

I turn down a
Blind alley

To run away
From forgetfulness,
Grief, longing and
The pins and needles
Of experience
I have gained

I throw myself off the
Bus, jam packed full of chickens
Clucking away about
The banality of
Their daily feed

I turn down
A blind alley
Hoping to meet
No one…
But myself

WHILST THE SEA SINGS PRAYERS

I am singing
Whilst the sea
Collects prayers
Settles to sleep
Unmoved by grief
I am not waiting
For it to sweep over me

I sleep whilst the
Sea sings prayers

SEAM LESS (I)

I let the thoughts back in ….
Like a wave sweeping under my door
I reached for the bottle, but it didn't stop them anymore
They had brought reinforcements from a dark and distant past
Marriages that had crumbled and a parent's love that didn't last
I let the thoughts back in
Because I was too weak to know
That I was somebody…
Even though you told me that wasn't so.

SEAM LESS (II)

I'm not sure when I started divorce proceedings
Against myself
Told him to get out
We're through, of all those false promises and lies.
You're ability to crush a butterfly
And complain it bite your hand.
I'm not sure I can stay with you...
Til the bitter end
I suppose...
I could take us down a pinch or two
And just try to be
Friends

SEAM LESS (III)

I have died
All my life
Under the stones
Of cold arms, whispering highs
Ending with an anchor around my feet
Plummeting…
Deeper and deeper...
Until I reach the skies

ON A BEACH, NEVER RETURNING (I)

I have nothing to regret now…
The moon knows my name
And even the trees are more welcoming here

I have nothing to leave now…
The jagged edges of the shore
Show me that each life can be split into

One moment
Together
Then all of a sudden
A pebble on the shore

I have nothing of myself now…
And that feels so much better than before.

ON A BEACH, NEVER RETURNING (II)

Just hold me here…

When the choppy waters get rough
When those that lay in wait to rip me up

Just hold me here …

In the clear blue sea
The jagged shore protecting me
The boat rocking me, into blissful calm

Just hold me here…
And don't let me go.

THE SHAPE OF ME

I'm trying to bend the day
Into the shape of me.
No flab over the belt
Or stray eye
Razor sharp focus
Bending the day
Into the shape of me.
Laughs, care
No shadow of doubt
No tinge of regret
I'm trying…
To bend the day
Into the shape of me.
Muscles…
To match the bank balance
Holding…
Whatever views
They want me to hold
Not thinking…
Just clapping with the crowd
I'm trying…
To bend the day into the shape of you.

METAMORPHOSIS II

I woke up with no distinguishing features…
Everything about me had been erased
I was just a tunnel of data that had seeped through my fingers
Clicks, ticks, likes, dislikes, pictures of cute cats and bombings all
rolled and rolled into one

I woke up with no distinguishing features…
Feeling or pain, everything aroused and disgusted me but I felt
none, it had pumped me into jelly
An experiment to see how far they could go
Could they eradicate my personality and just go where they told
me to go

I woke up with no distinguishing personality…
I held their views and attacked those that didn't
I bought at their shops
Eat where they eat
Tuning into their shows
Laughed and hated when they told me to

Then with a trembling finger, I switched myself off

THE SCREEN

Words flicker on the screen blocking out our dreams
They want more and more not nine hours but twenty spinning the
clock till we crawl on the floor
Words decay in front of our of eyes a meaningless babble cross
referenced and died
Then they lift our dying limbs to type a few more
Then leave our rotting carcass by the door

SEA AND KNOW

I look around myself
Never spending much time in..
Easier to cast my eyes
Than knowing how I got to this place that I take in

I look around
Sometimes the words lie too much with me
Calmer more relaxed they would take their place
Open doors see a happier side
See my inability to extinguish lies

See and know
That you can't take this picture from me
And God knows you tried

Because I have looked deep and around myself
And seen it here and now
That I'm glad to know you

RAGE RAGE AGAINST THE CASH MACHINE

£200 has just been swiped, Virgin, Sky, Orange or T - Immobile
£100 + late payment, service charges
And an extra £20 because we
F'in hate you

RAGE RAGE AGAINST THE CASH MACHINE

Then you take stock
It's only the 8th
10 days till pay day
When like hyenas they ripe open your dead bank account, again

And still there's a few days
For bills to bounce
Like pebbles skimming across the water
Plunging to new depths of despair

RAGE RAGE AGAINST THE CASH MACHINE

Socks will stay holy smelling of papal piss
The cat's litter tray will pile high
You will ask a beggar for small change
You will sneak a tin of beans through the check-out till

Rage Rage Rage
Against
The dying of the cash machine

THE DAY BEFORE WORK

All of a sudden the air becomes thin
And the glee of jumping out of work on Friday like a drunken
chimpanzee is gone
Instead the day becomes heavy…
Weighed down in disbelief that the minutes are ticking faster and
faster
"Surely it's not already twenty past three"
Then the evening falls, like a Transylvanian night
The gargoyles and wolves howling as you are passed your last
rites
David you will have to go to bed some time tonight.
Rocking to and fro in your captives bed
Starting at the clock till your eyes turn red…
Then you wake up like a coiled spring
Bounce down the street
Surprised to see that there is no one on your streets
Only to see it's only
Twenty past three… AM

SO MANY ARE FALLING FROM THE SKIES, OF COMFORTABLE LIVES

So many are falling from the skies, of comfortable lives
Until between the clouds, we can see me and you
Drinking in the bar one minute
Then outside Tesco
Mouths ajar

So many are breaking up inside
Falling from the skies,
Of comfortable lives

Passing the credit cards
Trying to grasp Universal Credit
Fingertips touching their children
On the way down
Landing with crash
At their door
Now repossessed
With someone else inside

So many are slipping through the cracks
Of this freezing land
Perishing in doorways
No hope insight
Except
Your hand

THE ISLAND OF THE DEAD

Under the soft snow of Alabama
They let him hang from a tree
To tell them "no one messes with Mary Lee"

In a classroom 50 miles south they picked on Maria Guadalupe.
And made her crawl on her knees

At a special school they broke off for tea, went back to their
dormitories
And saw Steve Jane and others too burnt to see

In the Island of the Dead
They made America cremate again

In the White House he sat petulant and cold
Letting loose
Women to be slapped
Muslims to be demonised
Black people to be murdered in the streets

But in the soul of the dead
America was great again

YOU DIDN'T PULL THE TRIGGER, BUT YOU DID (CHRISTCHURCH NEW ZEALAND)

You didn't pull the trigger, but you did

"I don't want immigrants
or those of a different race or creed"

I didn't pull the trigger, but you did

"the drip drip of my poison pen and lips
rips a storm of hatred in you"

Well…

You didn't pull the trigger, but you did

Each word, becomes a vile post
Each gesture, someone is pushed against a wall
Each speech a rallying cry to do more and more

You didn't pull the trigger
But your words did

THE HOKEY COKEY (BREXIT MESS-UP MIX)

You put David Davis in out
In Dominic Rabb, out, in Stephen Barclay
You shake them all about
You do the Hokey Cokey and you turn this country upside down
That's what it's all about...

Woah, the hokey cokey
Woah, the hokey cokey
Woah, the hokey cokey
Knees bent, arms stretched, let me out

You put your right wing in
The moderates out
In, out, in, out
You shake them all about
You do the Hokey Cokey and you've turned the country upside down
That's what it's all about...
Woah, the hokey cokey
Woah, the hokey cokey
Woah, the hokey cokey
Knees bent, arms stretched, let me out

You put Farage in, Boris too
Michael Gove and that bloody Mogg too
In, out, in, out
You shake them all about

You do the Hokey Cokey and you turn around and your country
is gone

That's what it's all about...

All together now
Woah, the hokey cokey
Woah, the hokey cokey
Woah, the hokey cokey
Knees bent, arms stretched, let me out

You put your party first
We want Boris out
In, out, out out out
You've shaken this country about
You do the Hokey Cokey and you turn against Europe
That's what it's all about...

Wait for it

Woah, we're going to live on beans
Woah, you're gonna steal your neighbour's peas
Woah, no medicines to heal
Knees bent, arms stretched, begging on the street

THE PATH BECOMES SLOWER (WW1 100 YEARS)

The path becomes slower…
The orders become louder
The constant din of shattering shells
Like pots and pans being washed and put away by you

My Mind becomes slower…
The generals clearly don't know what to do
I take a bullet carefullyfrom my friend's arm, as if I'm holding
you

My sleep has become numb…
The path to the other side has become shorter
Like the one I used to rush down to meet you

But now you hold the letter…
And it's not from me
Just ends with words
"Hold him in eternity."

DATING IN A STATE

I'm hanging around on a dating
In a state
Keyboards covered in tobacco, crisps, sticky with beer
Telling someone I like to climb mountains,
I'm calm and sensitive and in control
But I'm typing.. words …I can't ….see

And I'm starting to spill truths

"Divorced" "Kids"

"Oh "

I like betting, drinking, smoking ,doing most things to stop me thinking or feeling

"Mmm"

Kids miles away, and I'm up in the air

…………

Are you still there?

OVER AND OVER AGAIN

You couldn't type the keys you told me
Because your hand still hurt …
"Had you fractured it ?" I said
Forgetting my aching head that still hurt.

"I'm sorry" she said
Many many times
When my black eye was showing through
Covered up with our special friend "concealer"
"Let's forget" the bloodstained shirt too
The kick in the middle of the street
The scratches deep and permanently engrained

I kept on telling myself …
"it's me I blame"

If I did this….
Or said that …..
Was nicer then

The pain wouldn't come

But it did…..

Over
and over
 again

I WAKE UP COFFEE STAINED

I wake up coffee stained
Reach out for the first cig
The first cup
The first pair of clean clothes
No time for toast
The most I can hope for is that I make it through the door

I wake up coffee stained
Blurry eyed is this Monday or Thursday
June or July
Is it my father's birthday
No it can't be he died

I stumble for the train
Then realise I should be on the bus
As this is going to the place I should have been at yesterday
Let me go back to bed as I must

Be coffee stained
Blurry eyed
No use to man or ornament
I've officially decided this day has died

IN A BRIEF MOMENT

I've never
Seen a
Face
Fill up so quickly
 from the inside

The sheer mention
 of his father's name
brought a forced back
tear to his eyes

the teenage bravado,
 coolness slipped
and gone
in a brief moment
in one second in time
I saw..
A face fill up from the inside
Remembering
That his father..
 had died

IT IS A WINTER'S TALE

It's a cold night
Making this debt ridden country
Even more difficult to bear
grit is rationed
The street lamps turned off at night

And It's a cold night….

Making this even more difficult to bear
The elderly turn down e-ons of expensive gas
Workers wake up to see that their wages didn't last

And somewhere someone is not thinking of any of this….
The luxury Harrods candles bought and boxed off
Windows left open as the heating is put on full throttle
The bonuses on failed enterprises keep them secure and warm

But out of my window it's a cold night
And I really think someone might not make it through this night

But I doubt it's you…

MY FATHER'S WHITE HAND

I saw your white hand….
I never saw you look so peaceful
And happy
All the anger gone
All the pain
Withered away in your
White hand….

I said "I forgive you"
Saw a tear in your eyes
Body slipping away
No words
Just a closing of your door
No slamming any more

I touched your
White hand
more tender than before
and chose to forget all I'd locked away
as there's no point

as in life
as in death
to you I was no more . .

SWAN SONG

No life is right
No life is wrong
No life is left
With just a swan song

Somewhere along the life-line
You woke someone up
You made someone happy not fed up
And although you let people eat you up inside
You were too young to realise

That your life
Is not right

Your life
is not wrong

Your life was singing,
as it will at the swan song

THE HULA BALOO

I have a friend called the Hula Baloo
When my mum says "what did you do"

I say it wasn't me it was the
Hula Baloo

Sometimes my friend says
Rude words and spits
And doesn't eat his greens
Which make him feel sick

When I've splashed in a puddle
I know here comes trouble

But I have a useful friend..
If I've been naughty and don't know what to do
I say "it wasn't me "
It was . . .
The
Hula Baloo

GET SET GO

On your marks …..
    Get ready …..
        Go
           Back to bed
The world can just speed off
Gather momentum
Keep pace
I'll just
  Watch from the duvet the
   Safest place

Full speed ahead
Wiz round another
Tower block

No noise, sense or touch
Keep the windows firmly locked
Keep the cat close beside

Until finally the
Day hits gridlock
And I can see the drunkards round the bend
Hear the domestic THUD THUD
See the kids rip up
The playground, and
A can of strong lager tipped over my fence

On your marks get ready and
Go…………………………..

THESE LITTLE CHILDREN

These little children
Know none of this
The mothers' blood shot eyes
The terrible and whispering lie
As they sleep

These children should know none
Of this

Hanging around sharing
Laughs and life's long toys
Take cuddles to bed
See stars on the wall

But these little children see
All of this
Soak in cowardness
Grow thorns instead of wings

Need protection
Where there is none
Put their arms around a wicked lie

Grow fond of their discomforter
Laugh when they know they should cry
Take cuddles to bed
Yet again comforter

See the stars after
Another body blow

CHRISTMAS

We gathered round
And tucked into
Some family misery
(of that there were plenty)

Forgettable presents
Opened and discarded

A carving knife
For the vegetarian
A heavy metal CD
For the soul fan

We pulled crackers
(of which most of them were)
And left everything
Which had to be said
Unspoken

Slowly we crept
Back to our separate lives,
trying to forget
The misery that the others had caused inside

ALONE

I used to buy toilet paper
for 4 now just for one
so I get the 2 pack
the half loaf
the small pack of marge

Open the door of my
one bedroom flat
make a cup of tea for
One
listen to songs by people
missing someone

Make my single bed
turn round to see no one
wake up, kiss no one goodbye
shed tears that no one
will see

Come back at night, climb
the stone stair, open the door
turn on the light and imagine
you are there.

MOBILE PHONES

Do you remember the days before mobile phones?
when we used to talk to each other
without you looking at the screen
waiting for a text message to come through

Your importance measured by how often "it" rings
or the amount of numbers you have saved.

It's become a stranger in our bed
sort of chats you up
always lying between us
in the pub, café or club

Always demanding your attention,
care
checking if "he" has enough money
whether "he's" fully charged or a bit down
worried in case someone hurts,
or God forbid takes him away from you

So I join the queue
and text your phone
send a picture
send you an e-mail

This is what you want, a relationship
with no eye contact
or hands.

THE RIP BECAME A TEAR

The rip became a
Tear
That became a
Hole

That became a gap
That became a path
A road
 A motorway
  A river
   A crossing
    An Atlantic ocean
     A galactic hole

Since I could no longer
Say you were with me

AND IT'S A DEAD ONE

I'm turning over a new leaf
A dead one
Left over from autumn
Something unpleasant on this spring morning

I'm turning over a new leaf
And it's a dead one

STREET SCENE

That's a tanning studio
That's a chippy
That's a tanning studio

That's a hairdressers

Empty shop
Empty shop
Empty shop

That's a smoke free Wetherspoons

That's a closed pub
That's a closed pub
That's a closed pub

That's a couple strapped
for cash

That's a family next door
whose giro
couldn't last

That's a fake tan
That's a discarded chip paper
That's another fake tan

That's just a street
come to the end

ONCE

I was once in love you know
Although it was so long ago

Your bones barely covered in skin..
(your skin) hovering over my heart
Oh why did I let it start.

You sunk deep into your chair,
that distance in your eyes made me smile.
I thought your skin would break when
we made love; but it stretched and eased
                          as I teased.

Oh why are you like her,
even to the locks of your hair.

When awake you were alive:
            but then the silence.
The problems of the earth corroding
            your skin;
Oh why did it begin.

So young and pale, the blood eased
through your veins.
But your deep set eyes
held no surprise.

THESE WORDS YOU WILL NOT HEAR

These words you will not see
My face you will not touch
The chit chat of daily life not heard
My thoughts on the coming war unknown
The splinter in my finger untreated by
You

                         The clothes I wear unseen
                         The memory we could have shared

SO I MAKE IT UP

It was fabulous, interesting, a barrel full of laughs
We spent each day in each other's arms
and died together in the bath

JOSIE

Today from early mourning
I was with you…
From being woken with early morning dew of tears
To a frown that stuck to me like glue, hidden behind every word I
spoke

I miss you

5.30 am you came into my life
I carried you in my arms, walking past the park.
In the hours before I woke up
I held your little hand in mine
And breathed your skin like chloroform
Each passing child's face
Each pull on a mothers arm
Each father with child in tow
Each moment like this echoes back to me

You let her go…

Disposed of her in some kind of bin bag
Stuck, at the back of your mind

Today from early morning I was with you
Stuck to me like early morning dew

Something is missing

You

Snake River Crossing

The years seed the river
    With empty calendar dates
The speckled trout are not seen in, escaping
    Human minds.
Tongues of a thousand black cats
Lick the temporal seeds, aborting time
In the space of celestial moments
Revenant watchers do not speak of.
    Where they saw you
Is where minutes began, ticking silently
In auras of expiring days clinging
    To mossy creek logs
Your childhood feet once traipsed over,

    Never missing anything:
Never falling into those cold swirling
Pools where hours spun impatiently,
Waiting to drown out your poetry
    From rafts of undying rime.

Invisible Angels

If you go sideways tonight it's nothing new
    Beyond tattered bonds of being
        I wait for the saviors to return,
    Stamping out humanity's perfidy
        In homes, highways, & swap meet centers
    Where time is squirreled into the eyeball
        Of the no longer hidden machines
(Where our destiny unravels itself, cheaply:
"America is a demolition derby for social media
    Artists bemoaning the fall of low culture,"
        You tweet)…. All those
Wanting to reap wheel of fortune giveaways
    To sequester priceless fears in
Where guns are mightier than the mind's fingerprint
    Invisible angels toss horseshoes at,
Never coming close to the ultimate ring of fortune?
Plunge the knife in, Demon, so deeply these words
Break free from the addled spaces of my typing wend.
A human typo sees it all as the millennial joke,
    Cackling at our earth-bound foibles
    While sweeping ejecta of frazzled wings
(Abandoned by the landlady on her front porch),
You see how far dear Lucifer has fallen – again –
    From the hallowed space station

    Where my eviscerated halo remains,
Like accessories for some computer game casting
    Down the light of an unborn nova's heaven.

Terrestrial Re/visions

Unearthly as the coffin corners in rainbow glances, yes.
The striating blandishments linger as relics now
On the soiled sheets of History's bed,
& ramble through webs of parchment
    Becoming webs
Where the dethroned spiders of thought nestle
Imprisoned, waiting for another victim
    Like yourself.
This static energy abounds in plenitude
Along dust-fringed edifices of memory
    Where you last saw me
Picketing at the last rites for humanity,
Crushed on the supine ectoplasm
    Of lost desire.
Have another drink, shadowy scribes
Unwieldy as wordy Dickens, yes.
Where verbosity hangs in the balance
Of your weathered zeitgeist, taking
No measure beyond the ordinary

You must reach out to free the detritus
Ensnarled by these vowels & consonants
Before sundering the silken thread
Crisscrossing the universe of dread
Where this spidery scribe bleeds
    His tome of ink, rewritten
By the divine blogger's final cyber scrawl.

What Wields the Wind …When Speaking of Luna's Dress

It's just another day in a designer's paradise,
 Where everything is screwed-up dressed
Backwards in the mirror of cosmic pretenses.
 Lolling tonight on the precipice of dreams
I can accept death – but will the reaper redress me?

 Luna's lilac-patterned blue dress
Resizes itself in a backdoor retina, rippling out
A design without clear meaning. Light does not
 Rise against the crescendo of her daily being
To forgive the dress its faults, or the elements
  Fulsome as past gender obsessions.

 Beyond the eternal storm rainfall brings
To her fields razed by the lancing hoe
 Of seasons changing, beyond sunlight
What wields the wind in its bright ascending?

There are supposedly over 6,500 languages
  Thriving in diverse fashion
  On the human tongue, each one
Like a bee on the last unpicked flower on Luna's dress,
 From petals sprouting a song for wildflowers
  To pattern her nocturnal harvest.

Brains Dead Through Wisps of Fentanyl

When there was a spirit glowing thru nightfall
                In every vibe-being
Something unleashed in the scope of things,
                Unraveled itself
In another quiet majesty of thought
        Lingering – doggedly – despite the evanescent day
Dragging us down   with trifles,
All the after-effects of daily unrest
The media revels in: all just electronic prurience
& a taste for the banally depraved.
        Screw the Hollywood stars with their crash diets
Or the sex slaves of billionaires   & mortal morons
                Annoying you,
Old men with fast women tonight
Brains dead through wisps of fentanyl
                In the cranial sod
We'll dig up the remains of humanity
With anthropological aplomb,
        Recalling how beasts of burden once appeared
                With smartasses on Jeopardy.
They answered every damn question correctly –
Except why was the apocalypse a coming thing,
As unavoidable as herpes simplex in anal minds?
        When there was an idea in every human brain
The end seemed distant, beyond the reach
        Of those still building crosses
To impale our festering flesh on the dust
                Where no great thought stays.

Calling Forth a Specter Worn by Rhyme

I wish you were here right now, forgetting the centuries
                   & wayward dust
   My fingers slough through – remembering part & parcel
Of your forgotten rhymes ….   Yet hearing your voice on a
page
   More forceful than fading print, once in bold.
That's okay, the horror of time's severance is instructional.
Who yearns to do non-contemporary things: read wizened palms

   Your words become beneath the gaze of strangers
Briefly reaching out to the abyss   we remain in,
Enraptured by how your beauty of form   twisted itself
   Into a reliquary of mirrored dread, imparted
Always by the word-veins coursing through a retinal branch
Your pet Pangolin yearned to suck the blood from, before dying.
   Then leaving this carapace of existence

With you,   renouncing all its falseness   for the veil
Behind which jeweled sentences slip behind, for eternity' sake
Covering the gash   where our time-warped meeting lies
   Obscuring the final meanings of cool transgression:
These failed words emoting only a breath now
           Of syllables bookmarking us
In the afterlife   of non-verbal   shadows

Before Dying, It Drowns the Memory of You

I'd like to see the eternal options a little better creeping
Into the fabric of my being: Nothing will move me more
Than that circling night-hawk I used to see at Mountain's Edge
Going towards Pahrump,   or listening to songs
Whistled by desert predators in the sad nocturnes.
        Over memory's dust   I'll see a woman's handprint
Impressing the mountainside I've yet to climb,

In clear focus etching petroglyphs   inside the cavern
            Of my mortality waiting
Unlike yourself,   beyond the quietude   of prayer
When the lizard priests invoke the cleansing rain
(To re-christen history's   unclean rocks
Where the outlaw is more man than victim tonight),
& the Indian ghost women remember their children

Crying with coyotes sometimes in the unending night.
As the wind keeps moving between dust motes
            Vanishing everywhere,
With the eye-blink of nature watching you
The memory of love is sewn into the rock of ages
To plant seeds of ageless mortality there: perhaps
What songs of innocent trespassing voices succumb to.

Just Past Frenchman's Mountain

I have no eyes for the sun simmering in a mildewed body
Where a backwoods trail leads to a junction of desire
Fronting the darkness: behind there echoes
Of past & present voices impale your air.
(Chanting out a destiny of unsavory ends amid
The detritus I'll drunkenly bike over,

Where frustrations built into a litany of stone
To become old prayers no one hears at sunset.)
Not ill, nor in love with life any longer
While seeking a muse for the misbegotten,
And the landlady warned us stay out of the desert
& be content with the suburban jungle, yet who can?

The desert holds the found footage
Horror film of my existence:
Evidence of crime & punishment coming
      With a whirlwind's rainfall

Pattering over your long-buried shallow grave,
The chilling frame of your dismembered being.
When your supple skin turned ashen decrying
      The brunt of my untamed nature
Like the surrounding desert clime of brittle sage,
      & Native Indian spirit memories
Far beneath the peak our bodies never scaled
Keep us falling there, forever, into the mass grave
 With lovers of the orgy drumming the heart's genocide.

In the Cul-de-Sac of Dead End Lovers

Wending through the morass slowly desire melts you
Like stars being swallowed by the biggest black hole
          In the galaxy. The world is run on a base level
Of intelligence – or the lowest common denominator.
Female leaders are the coming wave & denounce male leaders
          As being the dumb asses we know they are.
(The times are not changing, burned out in their present tracks,
Making the past look more distant & the future unreachable
          While slighting the greatness of everyday life.)
Time's impromptu rush of devastating mileage
Scatters night into dead reckoning chased by the ride
          Of everyday existence consuming you
Through the perverse confines of everyday society.
Just taking leave of our senses before they take leave
          From our rites of gross nature unaccountably
Taking place on a non-existent pinhead, perhaps?

          See your Mother of Nod breastfeeding
The next personification of rot our magistrates decry,
& voters collapse in the eye of the ugly beholder at dusk
True believers dance in rapture over – while geek squads
Search for virgin bodies squirming in contraband joys!
Then who will blaze down some long highway's evil portal
The body politic snaps pictures of with terrestrial gloom

          Overclouding the dirty-bombed freeways
          Where mad drivers rear-end each other, until
Nothing wrecks your life tonight – except the truth crashing.

Beauty Ravished by Bulbs at Midnight

Just a lonely paparazzo in the neon-night
Brandishing the tools of the trade,
Until I saw Britney in her luxury car
The idea of her wearing underwear or not
Didn't matter much as an exposure theorem.
Because stunning beauty wins over abstract thought.
Especially that of any Rock trashy goddess
Sitting half-nude in a sleek BMW
Taking selfies of herself while parked outside
The Hard Rock hotel at midnight.
Flashbulbs pop incandescent shudders
Against her cool mafia hat & campy green
Shades reflecting Pop-mystical visions,
Including her sweating, now naked
Butt grinding bucket-seat vinyl,
Its gossamer shape spewing doubtless
Saliva of amour from perfect nether-lips
Hidden in slick vulva splendors.
Smiling because she's so fashionista
In the upper half-clothed part of her,
With brocaded transparent blouse
Barely concealing twin nipple implants.
Cry havoc through all the silent melodies
While we keep shooting film as bulbs flash,
Hoping for an instant exposure of her flesh
Equaling all the doves of vulgar paradise
Released by the creaming madrigals within her.

Flying, Dear Pegasus, Deep Into Your Hooded Hell

"Every whorehouse is childhood." – Kathy Acker

Is there a praying mantis seeking to unveil itself
In hyacinth remnants of your psyche when
The false bling of your soul is fool's gold?
Abandoned by elements you grimly turn
Into a recycled new Nintendo version
Of an invisible lesion between links
Haunting mired membranes so sweetly decaying
The foxfire of dreaming possesses you,
Between bouts with professional therapists.
Cold is my Lazarus lozenge inside you now
Across nova skin of spent molecules
Dancing their ion-footed way over the iambic
Umbilical cords strangling you so swiftly,
As time assumes its rumored obsolescence
No one must interfere with rapper Pegasus
Or hang an outsized necklace-clock
Around your Euro-trash lover's slit throat.
She who streams in a cyber-coma's way
Can only ride this pale galaxy's nag
Beyond the once fertile orbits of men,
Out from the anal cancers once shared
Where your body's better senses shine in
Acts of sweet debauchery on the half-shell.
Clutch your Barbie dolls before sacrificing them
To a renegade muse waiting to inveigle you
In lust's last flight of brain splatter now.

A Jailhouse Mausoleum

Mother Teresa looked good in tights
Were his final deathbed memories
Scribbled inside a matchbook cover
Given as an inheritance bequest
To some Vegas lounge lizards
Gluing pieces of his mental collage
For economic rip-offs (quite difficult)
Outside in the verdant garden of love
The landscapers unearth old bones
Of the jailbird's disliked guests
His pet Collie has pissed on for years
While the sun burns slowly out above
(Only six billion more years to go!)
All the unseen aliens get good tans
& the bedridden fallen patriarch now
Tries to see his life pass by in a flash
But instead it's just snowy interference
No Hollywood studio will ever film with
Digital leeches bleeding his green blood
For overnight deposits in Swiss banks
By nightfall they'll have his chalet-jail
Cleaned out of every untaxed bauble
Not even a sentimental spoon left
For the servants to polish or steal
Before the morning news obituaries
Declare the death of another billionaire.

Her Hip Skull & Crossbones

After all you've been through, cool Rocker babe,
Don't just jog on Italian beaches to bliss out,
Hoping to absolve that clunky love life

You wrote about in true confessions fashion.
Intercut then flesh-filled memories galore
Carving tattooed words with bobby pins

Into now rum-filled, buoyant breasts
Keeping you afloat in the trendy spas.
While sun-bathing you contemplate how

Virginia Woolf took her fatal ocean dip,
Disappearing into foaming currents
Oblivious to the true nature of sexual identities.

Meanwhile raucous punk music filters
Into your wavelength from a cliff-size radio,
Blasting out the country rawness of Rockabilly.

The social media misfits clucked tongues
At your whirlwind addictive love life
Portrayed on the cable news shows.

Now such brings the threat of wave-tears
Salty from an unseen sea within you,
& dampens the trendiness of fresh desire

On the outskirts of cool omniscience
You've swum to writing your lust lyrics,
Where only acceptable illusions remain

To decorate your sun-tanned skin with.
While taking a private sea cruise later
The drunken pirate waits for you in close-up,

Hoping to cleverly enslave you with tall tales
You will later embellish in your best songs
To trap in bottles floating to oblivion.

Shear

Rivaling the archives of time, her graying hair
Perpetually dyed still shimmers tonight
Under her stylist's caressing hands.
Daily a special flower is entwined there,
Until it unaccountably withers away

Through silken fragments, leaving petals
Spent like wan musical notes everywhere.
Watching her dress I will pause,
Savoring slow movements in sartorial detail:
How the bra is snugly fit, then clasped.

Time erodes with invisible precision;
On the mundane walkway outside
Life continues for limbs perambulating
After their descent from heavenly roots.
Just before dusk's encroaching haze

Comes a subtly enfolding grayness all
Pervading we fall captive to, in essence
Unable to hold it ourselves from night
Thrusting its dark blade inside us,
Shearing what we desire most.

Excerpts from a Rejected Novel

Pg. 23
Dispatches from hades are just measures
Of artistic creation when wind whitens
Prosy sidewalks with chalked dust clouds

Pg. 40
Skateboarders disappear nimbly into
Just shadows without good substance
This hatred of humans for one another

Pg. 52
Worse than a man without a country
& it's not whether you believe in god
But why god didn't believe in you

Pg. 60
While the discreet charm of opposites
Attracts all the feuding horny writers
Do press "1" for a taped Decalogue

Pg. 77
Prose like truth reeks of fabrication
Your major character confronts me
"The Author" with divine recriminations

Pg. 100
Now you "The Reader" please peruse
My climax of words for the artful apocalypse
Deleted now like humanity's last breath

Night's Amour in the Mob Museum

In the key of broken violin strings
    Sounding like zippers snapping off
To face the dead Mandalay Bay chorus, then
    Assaulted by jokes of a suicide bomber
Barfing out punch-lines with sickening zeal,
    Somebody tells you the world ended in a loo
Yesterday (after you received a butt-end call)
Giving you pinkeye, forever reciting dactyls.
    That's when your girlfriend materialized
With duct-taped, Spice Girl photopia;
    Where it's all done for the camera
(The sounds become squishy, a bad audio
Truncating the aural connections between
An experimental found footage interplay),
Beyond chic pansexually languid fetishism you'll
See 2 ghostly acolytes playing with strap-on plastic
Dildos slithering into a nude defecator's brainpan –
As one grunts in a duet for depravity's rainbow,
    Still wearing her gold-sequined high heels
    The camera zooms in & out relentlessly
While weird background music kicks in
The lyre worker kneels before her sister
Of obscene gyrations, braying, "Call Sappho!"
(… Ensconced on her brown-stained
      Porcelain throne while
Receiving the shoved-in, snaky host …)
You want to flush them both away
Before poetry   really happens.

After Filming Her Last Video of Sin City Nightfall

Camerado, do we cast out the whore

> Who ruined the apartment complex?

> Here in the sedate confines of normalcy,

Do we cast the first stones & unleash the dour

> Incantations roosting by her fallen silhouette,

> & brandish the ire of righteousness

At her boyfriend now, the hood brother

Who committed an unpardonable act of inhuman indecency?

Man's fall is no dream in this sun-seared-summer.

For the night is not young, Camerado,   & the bowels

Of deities preying on refuse   churn at such depravities

Where weeds sprout from the wire fences,

> & neighbors will later lay tribute dolls

> Erecting a memorial to the slain whore's baby

> (& the whore keeps working,   spitting out

A semen elixir   into the face   of bourgeois society

> Condemning her neighbors while they hide behind

All their platitudinous hypocrisies. During their last gala event

She played the craven queen spreading her anus for ghosts

reborn.

In their gangbang videos I watched the lone

Horror movie she starred in once,

Marveling at the baby's gruesome death scene to come,

Watching Lear's daughter croaking

In a spiritual death that bad acting failed to revive

With blonde bimbos   at defunct Playboy parties

As billionaires still choke   on the immaculate silk g-
stringed

Hair-pie strands of lovers   for the camcorders!

O, her pouting visage   smiles cattily into the lens

Until you touch her contoured soul of ebony

& tell her she's just a chrysalis now emerging

From chaos,   from a life so long corrupted

By the high-roller's sweet polyester cocoon, well-kept

(With all that it takes for scaling

The blackened ceiling

Of her apartment's now kitsch ruins)

As the diaphanous angels dressed in Gucci bold

Wait from a privileged distance pissing tears

To stain her old & broken cell phone images

Only the death of time distorts, quite the divine executioner

At her life's coming out costume party to die for.

Night Pictures of the Mind on a Fallen Pedestal

Renounce the glibness of facts unkind, she said,
Where nothing streams but splintered veins at dusk.
     In the clock-tower's overhanging
You'll see the specter of yourself   waiting
To paint old flesh   in ophidian shades.

But years later she asked me, "Out of what old lineage
Does the fine flesh crawl, across the highway
Leaving a snake's slick residue?
Artery akin to
A foul river awash
With my dead cunt squirting at god, just a little old man!"

With the looking glass of moments themselves fleeing you
Before foaming   over the bed someone slept on
She told me she couldn't leave the street,
Being homeless was better than swallowing dread
Hard as stone in the river of bedrock
     Our organs become.
   The night left
A cold ambience upon us   as telegenic images
Flashed by those trying to see our nudity.
To clothe our hurt with something dark is pragmatic
At best, to conjure up the dregs of fashion?
But really, it's only perennial unease
With what's underneath the fabric of existence,
Just more nothingness   in night's clothing.

Night Pictures in Thermal Colors

Poisons exit our pores X-pending
Waves of rainbow color-bytes
Far from black & white dilemmas
Historians confuse in debates

On America's race problem
While we interracial lovers giggle
& party like hip Rock stars
High as the unreachable infidel truth

Reeking of new wave perfume
Reality TV stars yearn to lick
From the anus of the last living god
Binding us to cave mentalities

Night melodies enslave your ears to
Porn sisters swearing they're not siblings
As ghosts of mediocrity haunt your cell
Saying "Press 911" before it's too late

Tumble My Acrobat Face Down on the Canvas

Speak to me old masters
Without blithe curses
The nocturnal winds course off beaches
Your childish harlequins delighted in
Traipsing merrily over
Erotic terrain the viewer can't quite see
For we're kept properly distanced
Out of respect for what circus performers suffer
During their harsh lives
Coupling in faint outlines with cheeks blushed
By omnipresent pink tones
Giving life to all before the many horses
Gallop past
Tumbling my acrobat
& saltant sort
Once in perfect equipoise with nature
& eternal sandscapes
Seeing the horizon disintegrate
In hastened time-lapse fashion
"Against the dark undazzled," quoting Wright
& other poets through my insolent haze
I watch the fermentation of humanity
With a cataract eye
I'll paste over darkness
One more time
The collage remnants of former lives
Viewed by disdaining apoplectics
In some royal manor

Damning the quagmire
Of elephants stomping your Madonna
Mother's face down on the canvas
Making bad artists of us all,
Sinful architects
Unable to devise
A new skyscraper for
An outmoded effigy
We're blind engineers unable to bridge
Gaps between ourselves
& let fossilization overtake
Our sands of dirty beaches now burning
The neon-scape night

For the reality
Of artful
Matter

Creates only
Anti-
Matter

Night Pictures of Old Bluesmen

(for Richard D. Houff)

You've played too many one night stands
In an era when rappers can't dig
Your sound's hip
Shatter of wail now
Across whiskey-drenched nocturnes
You don't need a weatherman for

All the scattered winds harping war
In a briefcase full of picks & delta echoes
Musty with a vinyl dark age.
Hey Bluesman, drowned by
Muddy waters & road gigs
Leading to nowhere lands

One inner city prosthetic hand claps
"It's the singer not the song,
The joint not the bong"
Bringing you down every time
In loose-lip raptures
Only the deaf can understand you

Now, at the journey's last bus stop
Waiting – & watching – where
A lost bum harmonizes, his back to the wind,
Chanting lyrics stolen by Rue blue heaven
… As the spirit of Bessie Smith
Turns the last bigot color blind

Winter's March to a Luxury Prison

How cold my night with its saviors sleeping,
& I'm blown away by beauty's imprint on a tortured road
I'm stumbling along, in winter throes,
Not caring how fate has gripped
    The shape of tomorrow.
In its hardly lambent claw
Caretakers wept to see the strangled throats
    Of their unreachable patrons.
Just another bad dream – perhaps
    Of my prosaic gray musing,
No doubt, seeing browbeaten ghosts all around me
Resembling rejects from a virtual reality game
Accessed via the Facebook creator's Oculus.
    Blood seeps beyond scarred tissue
Signifying the passion of all creation,
Even in a child's amazon eyes
    The commonplace is fascinating.
In the midst of these marching war criminals
    I feel more alive than ever;
In every damp stone a mundane jewel shines
As the heart opens anew with transplanted ambrosia,
Pumping systolic jolts to spin free
    Of mathematical logic.
In a short while I'll be one of the chosen,
    Cast into a palace for eternity,
Just another reborn victim hearing the sad entreaties
Of angelic vultures now awakening in dawn's light.

Nude Driving a Runaway Mustang

Car lovers everywhere "Rock Out!"
& hear the strangulating roadway thrust
Taking us past Dead Man's Curve
Where Jan & Dean serenade with guitar-licking
Lyrics sung-out in a lonesome culvert:
"Won't you come see me, Queen Jane?"
To an oblivious streaming traffic
You take a spangled bra off before
Some metallic onslaught time disdains
This ditch of gravedigger dreams
(Still as night dusting
A crash dummy's eyelid
For our tattooed tears),
No one forgets you're driving nude
Beyond diffracted flesh glimpses rife
With your last auto-erotic spasm
Hurtling us off Highway 61
To screams of Rockabilly heaven
We collided with walls of stone
Your ivory body flew up against
Offering its white tenderness
With climactic-controlled rhythms
Only the reborn dance to

On graves
Of unheard
Music

When Stephen Crane Courted His Bordello Madam

No one can fathom needing words
When nature directs the course of events
For this earthly vortex swallowing us.
Beyond that simian breed struggling
To pull us back deeply into the pit
Of old nightfall again, lightning wings
Through the firmament of lost desire.
To caress voids in the stricken beauty
We accept now with dogged strength?
Time breeds an army of marching stars

Beyond whatever fortune portends,
Bitterly or otherwise, in yellowing sky
A red badge of courage becomes wildfire.
There distant hawks hover over
The strewn bodies of Civil War dead

Naked as burned mimosa berries
On another plain, forgotten without
A mercy's remembered benediction.
It opens the door of longing too
In indescribable yearn for flesh mewling
From the prairie of jaundiced bones,
Loving the last morsel of each other
As wolves plunder a desert womb
His living passion slowly retreats from,
Bound by stillborn winter's heart.

The President Tweets His Betrayed Lover in the Midst of the Impeachment Inquiry

"… & by corrupting the fragile design of all matter,
Think of whatever virus it is   in animals
        Jumping greedily into the bloodstream of man.
Consider the macrophysics of some bold plan
        Beyond science & art:
All the little gods who can't paint out the sun
Observe the lily pinned   to the chosen's skin,
        Just a yellow heart on our chest
                As the trolls laugh
Teasing the luscious stalk of gender between us…!
We are the lotus eaters of a strange deflowering
        Swirling through the universe,
Undismayed by sentient suffering, yet
        Bound by laws we'll never accept.
I've always wondered, you know,
        About Thomas Jefferson & Sally Hemmings.
Did she discreetly place roses in her cleavage?
        With your alluring surety, I know
You don't feel the abiding chill all around us
Despite your treachery, but that's all right;
For the years separate us the way space does
        From the social media circus inferno we turn
The camera at, in a blinding light of factual truth.
Only here in the makeshift jungle
What remains are boring lawful rituals dividing
        What it was we loved between us,
Despised by all the hungry cannibals of priceless power
Indicting us illegally in a sold-out, Ship of State…"

Yearn for the Hologram's Dancing Girl with Night Tattoos

We wait in shadows, enamored of darkness
Rendering our forms sketchy presences
There, or not there, at night

Unafraid of bodyguards, their muscular girth
Or mean faces festooned by fight scars
Reeking of neighborhood wrath

We yearn for the hologram dancing girl's appearance
To blossom instantly in our midst:
All that we live for in tonight's sweet sighting

Of her familiar self *in the flesh* known
By heart, the impish face beauty morphs on
Despite the years passing all

In a dying acrobat's flying leap,
The lithe bodies of fallen angels & thieves
We desperately flail at with hungry hands

& shouts singing old ugly blues
For our transsexual dancing girl's beatifying scream
To harmonize with fallen embers, transformed

The Night of Reason Breeds Monsters

Darkness in the shape of dawn vanishes
Before the pale eyes of meteorologists,
What faces on the operating room floor can't see
As caustic shadows billow the dire either.
Invisibility remains an asset of the divine
I tell panhandlers outside on Main Street
Who reply, "Shit!" – & give me the finger.
I'm searching the sky for answers, Goya,
About our inexplicable distance from truth
(& other intangible unsightly elements?)
While the hospital receptionist smirks at me,
Wadding the Kleenex down her cleavage,
Reducing things to a common denominator.
We medical clinic picketers will still
Shake our fists at the malpractice labs
While waiting with assault weapons,
Concealed or otherwise, ready to strike
The black sun from synthetic heavens
Where immaculate births wait in test tubes,
Trying yet to conceive a master race….
I see the night of another day beyond you
Where hovering tragic spermicides grow
As embryos molder on your specimen tray,
Then slowly converge into cannibal fare
Suitable for the TV commercial gluttons
Who should eat what their asses expel.
Dark light will tint the last uncool cyber-byte
For the clinic's dead-again monsters to devour

Illusion of Love on the Parameter of Wizened Casemates

Wrapping the tin-foil goddess around your face
To taste the undiluted primal salt of past existence
The divine saliva mad people drink
Under the summer solstice pausing to saturate their sorrows

   I caress the dawn of original sin
   Like a beacon from otherworldly skies
   Skewered birds plummet now from
   Beating wings on the face of digital time

Stricken by the clock without prefabricated hands
You reach to enfold the Void with prepubescent graying shades
& shape the found evidence of dying reason into The Effigy of Art
Forms of postnatal lusting forms now gather carefully around

   What remains of the blistered canvas?
Nothing more dampens the pit of my lost self-esteem
But self-pity to see lost reverence reflected in somas dim
Clustering there (on your forehead) with irrefragable zygotes
In order to quiet the coming shades

Savior of History

Nothing can ravage the pit of my flagging self-esteem
Like your hand on the abyss of migrant faces
Your crepuscular shadow clusters with faux-compassion around:
With lunar projectiles coursing from your eyes
To ravish the lingering puffs of springtime hope
The true nature of diverse hatreds enveloping   what stalks
the night
Via my lost geography's eroding dominion   over you:

    & my life, old folly imperious
    As it seems?   With blood-rife
    Passions horrific to the mind's eye
    You seek to pluck from me
    While I sleep with artificial roses
    Beneath the tainted bedsheets
    The ardor of escaping their banishment of second sight

Regales the spinster watching us   wanting the parallel
Universe to part ways   forever   from us
My mad optometrist says will be imploded in mote-like
Visions from the beginning of time just snapping its self-portrait
Of what will remain beyond the colossal brain's blinding
               Of an old god's artificial ignorance:

No One Has Slept with Night & Lived to Tell About It on Unsocial Media

Unless you count those who are pariahs among us   shivering –/
I remember wondering about Chris Burden in art school,
how he slithered
Through the night darkly   cutting his flesh to red Remington
ribbons
While the nubile onlookers of lewd imagination giggled at
Arakawa's words
Stenciled on invisible foreheads: simply the brunt of humanity
Reporting live   from the other side   of the
plundered moon
While so many   find it so hard   to just live on earth,

     The moonlight fades here   as it does tonight in Iraq
Bringing us to the moments of discontent words cannot form
bridges to:
     All that we constructed in the ruins of nature & art
Haunt the piecemeal leftovers of generations past   still hugging
     Our maleficent airs.   Those trolling through slivering
waters
The shrapnel of what we make and unmake devolves all being
into,
     Whoever fought back the lure of eternity (yet //
               Must yet succumb to it —)

I remember wondering about great painters & valiant wielders
     Of pen or pencil re-defining   the shape of us
In the caustic lens (later)   of electronic enhancement,
X-raying the underside of   irruptive surgical veins

In the finest detail,   O photographic realism of bloodlust
Spilled in the antiquarian   fastness of our digitalized abodes

I wonder no more in, for the death of art will overcome time
Before we are reborn in the true light's color of darkness …///=

Unearthing a Dark Harvest for the Birthday of Gods

Dawn unfurls its edifice of light to dismay me: to enrapture minions of earth
Before the second coming of humanity,   wherein my empty dark bottle vanishes
& I'm sober again with the picturesque fractal morning.
          Now lost children rise from the surrounding faint staleness
To see all that's been bequeathed   to the shadowing scorpion
Beneath them.   Feeding on rhyme's   lost reason
For a tableau waiting to be painted,   they play within its boundless frame
Like a puerile pigment of flesh & blood   smearing   the countryside of dreams

Where no god comes;   for only in monochromatic strokes of divine color
Will they ever see   their limbs growing   again/// =?

(If you must renounce them, do so with cautionary grace
Conforming to the rules of a civilized society:
Sprinkle stardust from Pleiades over them as well,
For they are the divine fodder for the coming soil
Where there are no sad rows of sameness)

Within the straight arrow's path
                    From wherever it was
                                        Night made them

In the Hothouse of Virgins Words Burn

The countless moments of pansexual intimacy
    & forbidden acts in the hothouse of Virgins
Recall lewd and hidden sonnets beneath a celibate's love trove.
    Just imagine the new Victorians becoming trans-lovers
In futuristic America where anything goes.   It's a crime to be
straight:
Spirits touching the sweating porcelain brow of Keats
    On his otherworldly death bed
Will find their passion on a disintegrating comet's tail
In the supernova heavens of broken hearts devouring
    The last Virgins banished from earth,
All those resisters of the land's viral polyamorous airs
Where the laws cremate those old literary throwback bodies
    On planets of ash:

For to turn back the dark pages of history
    Some must remain blindly illiterate
    To the inevitability
That minority Virgins will always exist alongside us,
Reading their outlawed romantic authors of spiritual love

While their impassioned words burn like genders turning
    On the spit of crucified bodies.

The Last Word

1.
The lies of modern times
Overwhelm those of greater antiquity,
Propelling all words media-wrought
Into a common electronic dram-thought
Sometimes devoid of meaningful outcome.

2.
Outside the realm of verbal para-physics
Must linger the truth of sorts, medley
Of titanic retro-propulsions
Parsing currents aqua-wrung –
Remains like underwater petroglyphs
Swallowed whole by Melville's whale
Or etched on its innards in 5G retina color-
Bytes that pixilated Ahab's eyes
To scribble lines around a blowhole spouting
     The Word
(At long last the coming of fish prophets!)

3.
On Baghdad streets of nightfall blood
A dark waif-woman wanted to shout
The truth of all lies from broken teeth,
Then raze treachery beyond eruptions
Accompanying music with rocket glare.
Tell of her desire's eradication of thought
Beneath the fine-veined skin those brutal hands
Of stray soldiers in raping, singed –

While you, a continent away,
Banished her screams with rationalizing rhetoric
Never whispered on tongues of missing dead.

The Model Muse in Nu-Wave Purgatory

Dope video game: downloading pics to reveal our sister
        With all the unsightly blemishes to come, perhaps
                        Mocking your virago wife
Behind Belgian lace. Her remolded breasts following double
mastectomy
        Were enhanced by a soft-focused embellishing
My illustrious photography never did justice to....   I remember
Our private Euro-odyssey, still fantasizing with nagging memory

All the majesty of cathedrals plus their art   casting our bodies
In otherworldly postures Giotto once painted.... Unenlightened,
We left that venue for more earthly roads,   finding the waters
Freeing our dreams from booze with a magician's oceanic elixir.
All that I needed one day gazing into the Bellagio's hotel depths
I heard unknown voices crying for the lute, not the heavy metal
        Of your Rock music blasting outside on tourist radios,
Impinging on our grunge eardrums wrinkled by morning's first frost

As feeding blackbirds dashed with their straw burdens
Through invisible eyes of statuary gods.
Sounds meshed into a strange symphony while fishermen angled in
Your mind, hoping to hook our alluring, trans-sexed sister?
Meanwhile hidden Movado aquatic watches recalibrated
The silent steps of creatures devolving backwards beneath us,
                Wanting to take dear sister from us,
Though nothing beckoned enough beyond her seaweed's shadow
To mar the graven images I write these picturesque lyrics to....

See her last close-up? She screams now, sabotaging
The medicine cabinet with a claw hammer, while in her dream
You pull the plug on Mother in the ICU ward
        Time floods invisibly
                In a warped eye-blink
                        Gone from hoary flesh
"Let me cup her sagging implants," you say
        Doctors cannot bottle for posterity
                Her legal poison
To sell dark net freaks searching for satori,
        Freeing them from tyranny-of-tourism
                Or fears of not losing weight
With the latest strap-on belly shaker:
                I see our sister
                        Surfing dream-webs

        In my penultimate abstract montage of her
Hanging upside-down   on the fringes of mass medulla –
        A gallery of night shots
        (& shadows)

Where her face remains the steady mocking refraction
        Forging my impudence
                For wearing her bra.

Night Poets Speak to Lorca When Lights Are Low

Renegade poets are everywhere muzzled
By oppressive laws & their mercenary infidels
Clinging to the bough of corporate drivel,
With little wisdom born of creative downturn.
Nor the truth of anything beyond what
Dead ghost writers with digital teeth
Bite you with in the heat of the night,
When you're alone trying to write
A passable suicide note in fresh blood
Seeping from a jagged flesh wound
Anemic plastic surgeons can't stitch
Up your behind when your credit is *mal,*
& a nude Christ dances through dreams.
Another home invader, perhaps, to return
Beyond all the decaying aesthetic morals
You once rescued the reading public from –
A born again tormentor forever haunting
Any poet synching the line of truth with
The artesian fountains of bygone basilicas:
Just a redacted mantra for the unseen
As Sappho weeps in TV closets tonight
Invaded by freakily tousled pitchmen
As the night veers toward infinity.
Ghost soldiers play with children's bones
While I channel surf your mind endlessly,
Watching everything – or nothing –
Glide through tenured old commercials.
We've bled from moments of total greed:

Unable to afford art's truth or consequences.
As a result we molder in history's plunder
For pre-Columbian art slowly fading on
Video screens static in our infected souls
With malice to come.   Still I am not
A judging overseer of the way things are,
As night overlaps something beyond physics
Threatening to keep us from falling upright.
Later I'll turn to my boyfriend with a vial,
Taking his saliva as holy water to sprinkle
On the remains of censored memories
Inside my tomb's unbearable whiteness.

Walking Naked Through My Mind

1.

Your bikini became a catwalk shroud
Wrapped lovingly around my throat
During those times away from you.
Outside on the porch, not even
The wild birds we used to feed
(Even the black crow you said
Was your self-portrait from Van Gogh?)
Console me of times past forgetting.
Listening to atonal jazz, I pace the floor
     & ponder ingenious ways
     To dismember grief spaces
In homage to your phantasm I see
Walking naked through my mind.
Do I deserve some ectoplasmic Orb –,
With its piquant, even briny smell
Flooding my nostrils at all hours?
You drowned five years ago because
You couldn't swim from a carnival
Cruise all the way to Finland.
The sea bloats your memory
For the marine birds to peck at,
That flesh I'll never hold again
     In the possessive way
     You once scorned:

2.

<"imagine if we become a nation of nudists,
Unvarnished by hypocritical coverings,

Veneers, smokescreens, & techno-speak
Wouldn't life be so blunt? Even

Painful to all the earth's liars;
For to clothe something is pragmatic

At best, but what constitutes fashion?
Garments the living wear get ticklish,

& artful beyond the mere political
Changes cover-ups are heir to

When we show something pubic
One day, then publicly the next –

All supposedly reflecting fickle tastes,
But really it's just perennial unease

With what's underneath the diaphanousness
Of existing," > U-text from unknown coral reefs//…

3.

Yet outside my window
The crows circle now
For the morning morphs itself
Into an invisible *deus ex machina*

Of another noon
The desert heat absorbs thirstily.

I begin to sketch a pecking orgy
Of marine predators attacking you,

Lapsing into a pantheistic wonder
… While my pencil moves

Spider-like across desolate rocks
Under which nothing is written

    but
           your
                shadow